10 Easter Bunny Stories

Table of Contents

The Easter Bunny's Special Delivery

Once upon a time, there was a little girl named Sophie. Sophie loved Easter it was her favorite holiday. She loved decorating Easter eggs, hunting for Easter eggs, and most of all, she loved getting Easter gifts from the Easter Bunny.

Sophie woke up early on Easter morning and ran to the living room to see if the Easter Bunny had left her any gifts. To her surprise, there was a big box wrapped in shiny Easter paper sitting in the middle of the room. Excitedly, she opened the box to find a beautiful Easter dress, a matching hat, and a pair of shiny shoes.

Sophie was thrilled with her gifts and couldn't wait to put them on. She put on the dress, hat, and shoes, and twirled around the room, feeling like a princess. She looked in the mirror and saw that she looked like a beautiful Easter fairy.

But then, Sophie noticed a note inside the box. It read: "My dear Sophie, these are not just ordinary gifts, they are magical. With these gifts, you will be able to travel to the Easter Bunny's special garden. There, you will find the most beautiful Easter eggs you have ever seen. But, be careful, you only have until sunset to find the golden egg, otherwise, the magic will be gone and you will not be able to come back."

Sophie was excited and scared at the same time. She didn't know if she would be able to find the golden egg in time. But she knew she had to try. She closed her eyes and focused on the garden. Suddenly, she felt a warm breeze and when she opened her eyes, she found herself in a beautiful garden filled with colorful flowers, and Easter eggs of all shapes and sizes.

Sophie ran around the garden, looking for the golden egg. She found eggs in all colors and shapes, but none of them were golden. She was running out of time, and she began to feel discouraged. But then, she saw a beautiful butterfly flying towards a bush. She followed the butterfly and found the golden egg hidden among the branches.

Sophie picked up the egg and held it tightly. Suddenly, she felt a warm breeze again, and when she opened her eyes, she was back in her living room. She looked at the clock and saw that it was just a few minutes before sunset.

Sophie was so happy she had found the golden egg and the magic had worked. She looked at the dress, hat, and shoes, and smiled. She knew she would always remember this special Easter and the magical gift from the Easter Bunny.

From that day on, Sophie knew that Easter was not just about getting gifts, it was about the adventure and the magic of the Easter Bunny. She would always remember the day when she traveled to the Easter Bunny's special garden and found the golden egg.

Easter Morning Surprise

Once upon a time, there was a little boy named Max. Max was an adventurous boy who loved to explore the world around him. He loved going on hikes, playing in the woods, and discovering new things. But what Max loved the most was Easter, and the Easter egg hunt that was organized every year in his neighborhood.

One Easter morning, Max woke up early, full of excitement for the egg hunt that was about to take place. He quickly got dressed and ran outside to join the other children who were already gathered in the park.

The Easter Bunny had hidden eggs all over the park, and the children were given baskets to collect as many eggs as they could find. Max was determined to find the most eggs and be the winner of the egg hunt. He ran around the park, searching for eggs behind bushes, under trees, and in the most unexpected places.

As the hunt went on, Max found more and more eggs, but he noticed that something was different this year. The eggs he found were not the usual plastic eggs filled with candy, they were real eggs. He was puzzled, but he kept searching.

Finally, Max found the last egg, and it was a golden one. He opened it, and inside he found a note. The note read: "Congratulations, Max! You have found the golden egg! You have won the Easter egg hunt. But the real prize is not the eggs you have found, it's the adventure you have been on. Follow the clues to discover the real Easter gift."

Max was curious and excited, he read the first clue: "The first step to finding your prize is to look up." Max looked up and saw a hot air balloon floating in the sky. He read the second clue: "The second step is to find the basket." Max looked around and saw a basket hidden among the bushes. He read the third and final clue: "The last step is to climb aboard and enjoy the ride."

Max climbed aboard the hot air balloon and took off. He floated high in the sky, taking in the beautiful view of the city below. As he soared above the clouds, Max couldn't believe his luck.

He had never been on a hot air balloon before, and he never expected this to be the Easter gift he would receive.

As the hot air balloon journeyed on, Max noticed that the Easter Bunny had set up a picnic for him on board. There were sandwiches, cookies, and juice, and Max was delighted to enjoy a meal while flying.

The Easter Bunny had also left him a gift, a book of adventure stories, and Max couldn't wait to read them. He knew this would be the perfect way to keep his adventurous spirit alive all year round.

As the hot air balloon journey came to an end, Max landed back on the ground, still in awe of the fantastic experience he just had. He thanked the Easter Bunny and couldn't wait to tell his family and friends about his Easter morning adventure.

From that day on, Max's love for adventure only grew stronger and he knew that the Easter Bunny had given him a gift that he would treasure forever. He looked forward to the next Easter and the adventures that it would bring. He knew that with the Easter Bunny, anything was possible and that the real gift was not the hot air balloon ride, but the memories and experiences that came with it.

The Easter Bunny's Egg Hunt Adventure

Once upon a time, there was a boy named Timmy. Timmy loved Easter, but what he loved most about it was the Easter egg hunt. He would spend hours searching for eggs and trying to find the golden one that would win him the grand prize.

This Easter, Timmy woke up early and couldn't wait to start the hunt. He put on his new Easter outfit and ran outside to join the other children in the park. The Easter Bunny had set up an egg hunt like no other. It was an adventure egg hunt, and the children would have to solve clues and complete challenges to find the eggs.

The first clue led Timmy to a tree where he found a small basket with a map inside. The map showed a path that led to the first challenge. Timmy followed the path and found a rope bridge that he had to cross to get to the next challenge. He was a little scared but he was determined to find the eggs.

The next challenge was a maze made of bushes. Timmy had to find his way through the maze to find the next clue. He was getting a little frustrated, but he kept going. He finally found the clue that led him to a cave. Inside the cave, he found a chest with more clues and a flashlight.

Timmy followed the clues, and they led him to a river. He had to use the flashlight to find a hidden path that would lead him to the next challenge. The path was narrow, and Timmy had to be careful not to fall in the river.

The next challenge was a treasure hunt. Timmy had to find a key that would unlock the chest with the eggs. He searched high and low and finally found the key hidden under a rock. He unlocked the chest and found a golden egg and many other colorful eggs.

Timmy was so happy he had completed all the challenges and found the golden egg. He ran back to the park to show the Easter Bunny his prize. The Easter Bunny was impressed with Timmy's determination and gave him a special prize, a trip to a real adventure park where he could have the adventure of a lifetime.

From that day on, Timmy loved Easter even more, not just because of the eggs, but because of the adventure that came with it. He couldn't wait for next Easter to come and see what kind of adventure the Easter Bunny had in store for him. He knew that with the Easter Bunny anything was possible, and that the real gift was the memories and experiences that came with it.

A Gift from the Easter Bunny

Once upon a time, there was a little girl named Sophie. Sophie loved Easter, but what she loved most about it was the chocolate bunnies. She would always look forward to the Easter Bunny bringing her a big chocolate bunny every year.

This Easter, Sophie woke up early and couldn't wait to see what the Easter Bunny had brought her. She ran to the living room and found a big chocolate bunny on the table, but there was something different about it. It was a real bunny, a live one!

Sophie was so excited she had never had a pet before. She picked up the bunny and held it close, she knew she had to take good care of it. The Easter Bunny had also left her a note, it read: "This bunny is yours to take care of, but don't worry, I'll be back to check on you both."

Sophie was so happy, she had a new best friend, and she couldn't wait to take care of it. She named the bunny Coco, and they became inseparable. They would spend their days playing in the garden and exploring the neighborhood.

One day, the Easter Bunny returned, and he had a surprise for Sophie and Coco. He had planned an adventure for them. He took them to a nearby forest where they could explore and have fun.

Sophie and Coco had the time of their lives, they climbed trees, swam in a lake, and even had a picnic. They saw so many animals and plants that they had never seen before. Sophie was so grateful to the Easter Bunny for giving her and Coco this wonderful experience.

As the day came to an end, the Easter Bunny took them back home, but not before giving Sophie a special gift. He gave her a book about the forest and all the animals and plants they had seen. Sophie was so excited to learn more about her new favorite place.

From that day on, Sophie loved Easter even more, not just because of the chocolate bunnies, but because of the adventures that came with it. She couldn't wait for next Easter to come and see what kind of adventure the Easter Bunny had in store for her and Coco. She knew that with the Easter Bunny anything was possible, and that the real gift was the memories and experiences that came with it.

Benny the Brave: A Easter Bunny's Tale

Once upon a time, in a far-off land, lived a young bunny named Benny. Benny was different from all the other bunnies in his colony. He was small, shy and timid, and often felt out of place. He didn't have the same energy and enthusiasm as the other bunnies and often felt left out.

One day, while out foraging for food, Benny stumbled upon a mysterious cave. Being a curious bunny, he ventured inside and discovered a magical world of Easter eggs, chocolate treats and colorful ribbons. Benny was amazed and couldn't believe his eyes. He had never seen anything like it before.

As he explored this magical world, he heard a soft voice calling his name. He followed the voice and found an old, wise Easter Bunny, who was the guardian of this magical place. The old Easter Bunny explained to Benny that he was chosen to be the next Easter Bunny and that it was his destiny to bring joy and happiness to all the children in the world.

Benny couldn't believe it. He, little old shy and timid Benny, was chosen to be the next Easter Bunny? The old Easter Bunny saw the skepticism in Benny's eyes and assured him that he had everything it takes to be a great Easter Bunny. He just needed to believe in himself and find the courage within him.

Benny was hesitant at first, but the old Easter Bunny's words resonated with him. He realized that he had always wanted to make a difference and bring joy to others, but he had never had the courage to try. But now, with the old Easter Bunny's encouragement, he knew that he could do it.

From that day on, Benny began to train with the old Easter Bunny, learning everything there was to know about Easter eggs, chocolate treats and colorful ribbons. He practiced hopping, running and hiding eggs, until he became the best Easter Bunny in the colony.

On the day of the Easter celebration, Benny put on his Easter Bunny suit, took his basket of eggs and set off to deliver them to the children. At first, he was still shy and timid, but as he saw the children's faces light up with joy and
excitement, he knew that he had found his true calling. He was finally the Easter Bunny he always wanted to be.

From then on, Benny became known as "Benny the Brave" and was loved by all the children in the land. He continued to bring joy and happiness to the children every Easter and was always remembered as the Easter Bunny who found the courage within him to make a difference.

And that is how Benny the Brave, the once shy and timid bunny, became one of the most beloved Easter Bunnies of all time. He proved that no matter how small or timid you may feel, with a bit of courage and determination, you can accomplish great things and make a difference in the world.

Bunny's Easter Basket

It was the day before Easter, and all the children in the neighborhood were excited for the big day. They had heard rumors that the Easter Bunny had a special surprise for them this year. Little did they know, the surprise was not just for them, but for the whole community.

Charlie, a young boy who loved Easter, was determined to find out what the surprise was. He asked his friends and even asked the Easter Bunny himself, but no one would tell him. Frustrated, he decided to take matters into his own hands and set out to find the surprise on his own.

Charlie's adventure began early in the morning. He set out on his bike and followed a trail of Easter eggs that seemed to lead him out of the neighborhood and into the countryside. He rode for miles, following the trail until he finally reached a big, beautiful farm.

As he approached the farm, he saw the Easter Bunny hopping around, surrounded by a group of children. The Easter Bunny saw Charlie and called him over. He explained that the surprise was a special Easter egg hunt on the farm, where the children would get to learn about where Easter eggs come from and how they are made.

The children were excited and couldn't wait to start the hunt. The Easter Bunny divided them into groups and gave each group a map and a basket. He explained that the eggs were hidden all over the farm and that they would have to solve clues and complete challenges to find them.

Charlie's group set off on their adventure. They visited the chicken coop and learned about how eggs are laid. They went to the barn and learned about how Easter eggs are decorated. They even got to help decorate some eggs themselves.

The children searched high and low, following the clues and completing the challenges. They found eggs hidden in the haystacks, in the pond, and even in the trees. And finally, after hours of searching, they found the golden egg, hidden in the Easter Bunny's burrow.
The Easter Bunny congratulated the children on their success and rewarded them with a special Easter feast. The children sat down to enjoy a delicious meal of roast lamb, mashed potatoes, and, of course, Easter eggs.

But the best part of the day was yet to come. The Easter Bunny had one more surprise for the children, he had arranged for them to take some of the eggs back home with them. The children were thrilled, they had not only had a great adventure, but they also had eggs to take home and share with their families.

Charlie returned home that night, tired but happy. He had not only found the Easter Bunny's surprise, but he had also learned about where Easter eggs come from, and how they are made. He knew that this was a Easter adventure he would never forget.

The Easter Bunny's Lost Treasure

Once upon a time, in a magical forest filled with colorful flowers and singing birds, lived the Easter Bunny. He was known for delivering Easter eggs and gifts to children all over the world on the night before Easter Sunday. But, there was one thing that made the Easter Bunny different from all the other bunnies in the forest. He had a special treasure that he kept hidden deep within the forest.

One day, while the Easter Bunny was out delivering Easter eggs, a group of mischievous raccoons stumbled upon his secret treasure. They took everything and scattered the treasure all around the forest. The Easter Bunny returned to find his treasure missing and he was devastated. He knew that he had to find the treasure before Easter Sunday, or the children would wake up to empty baskets.

The Easter Bunny set out on an adventure to find his lost treasure. He asked all the animals in the forest if they had seen anything suspicious, but none of them had. Just when the Easter Bunny was about to give up hope, he met a wise old owl who told him of a legend about a magical map that could lead him to the lost treasure.

The Easter Bunny followed the owl's instructions and found the map deep in the forest. The map was ancient and written in a language that the Easter Bunny could not understand. He knew he needed help to decipher it. The Easter Bunny gathered all of his animal friends and together, they set out to find the lost treasure.

They encountered many challenges along the way, from crossing a treacherous river to escaping from a cave filled with bats. But, with the help of his friends, the Easter Bunny was able to overcome each obstacle. Finally, they reached the spot marked on the map, and there it was, the Easter Bunny's lost treasure

The treasure was filled with Easter eggs of all shapes and sizes, chocolate bunnies, and other Easter gifts. The Easter Bunny was overjoyed to have his treasure back. He thanked his animal friends and promised to share the treasure with them. Together, they returned to the forest, and on Easter Sunday, the children woke up to find baskets filled with Easter goodies.

From that day on, the Easter Bunny's treasure was no longer a secret. Every Easter, the animals and the Easter Bunny would gather together and share the treasure with the children. And, the legend of the Easter Bunny's lost treasure became a beloved tale passed down from generation to generation.

Easter Bunny's Sweet Treats

Once upon a time, in a small village nestled in the heart of the forest, there lived a young boy named Jack. Jack was an adventurous and curious child, always eager to explore the world around him. He had heard stories of the Easter Bunny and how he would bring gifts to children on Easter Sunday, but he had never seen the Easter Bunny himself.

One day, as he was wandering through the forest, he came across a strange and mysterious cave. Without hesitation, he decided to investigate. As he made his way deeper into the cave, he heard a faint rustling sound. Suddenly, out of the shadows emerged a small, fluffy rabbit with a large basket of Easter eggs.

The Easter Bunny looked up at Jack with a friendly smile. "I have been watching you, young one," he said. "I can see that you have a great spirit of adventure and curiosity. That is why I have chosen you to be my helper this Easter."

Jack was overjoyed. He had always wanted to meet the Easter Bunny and now he had the chance to help him deliver gifts to children on Easter Sunday. The Easter Bunny gave Jack a special suit and a map of the village, and together they set off on an adventure to deliver Easter eggs and chocolate to all the children.

As they made their way through the village, Jack helped the Easter Bunny sneak into the homes of the children, leaving Easter eggs and chocolate in the most unexpected places. The children were delighted to wake up on Easter Sunday and find the Easter Bunny's gifts.

Jack and the Easter Bunny continued their journey for the whole day, until every child in the village had received a gift. As the sun began to set, the Easter Bunny turned to Jack and said, "You have done a great job, young one. I am very pleased with your help. You have shown great courage and kindness, and I will never forget it."

With that, the Easter Bunny disappeared into the forest, leaving Jack with a heart full of memories of his adventure and a newfound sense of courage. From that day on, Jack knew that no matter what challenges he faced, he had the courage and determination to overcome them, just like the Easter Bunny.

The Easter Bunny's Treasure Hunt

Once upon a time, in a magical forest, there lived the Easter Bunny. He had a special talent of hiding Easter eggs and treats for all the children in the forest to find. Every year, the Easter Bunny would hide Easter eggs in the most unexpected places, making it a treasure hunt for the children.

This year, the Easter Bunny had a special surprise for the children. He had hidden a golden Easter egg, the most valuable egg of all, and whoever found it would receive a special gift from the Easter Bunny himself. The children were very excited and couldn't wait to start their treasure hunt.

The Easter Bunny gave them a clue to start their treasure hunt. The clue read: "The golden egg is hidden in a place where the sun shines bright, and the water runs high." The children thought about it for a moment, and then set off to find the golden egg.

The first child to set off on the treasure hunt was a little boy named Jack. He thought that the clue might be leading him to the river, so he headed to the river. He searched high and low, but he couldn't find the golden egg. He thought that maybe he was wrong, so he decided to go back to the Easter Bunny and ask him for another clue.

The Easter Bunny gave Jack another clue: "The golden egg is hidden in a place where the birds sing sweetly and the flowers bloom." Jack thought about it for a moment, and then set off to find the golden egg. He went to the forest and searched for a place where the birds sang sweetly and the flowers bloomed. He searched for hours, but he couldn't find the golden egg.

Meanwhile, another child named Emily set off on the treasure hunt. She thought that the clue might be leading her to the meadow, so she headed to the meadow. She searched high and low, and she finally found the golden egg. She was so excited that she ran back to the Easter Bunny to show him the golden egg.

The Easter Bunny was very happy and proud of Emily for finding the golden egg. He congratulated her and gave her a special Easter basket filled with treats and goodies. Emily was very happy and thanked the Easter Bunny for such a wonderful treasure hunt.

From that day on, the Easter Bunny's treasure hunt became a tradition in the forest. Every year, the children would set off to find the golden egg, and whoever found it would receive a special gift from the Easter Bunny. The treasure hunt became a fun and exciting adventure for the children, and it brought joy and excitement to the forest.

Easter Bunny's Magic Eggs

Once upon a time, in a magical forest, there was a kind and gentle Easter Bunny named Peter. He lived in a cozy burrow with his wife and children, and every year, he would travel far and wide to deliver Easter eggs to all the children in the world.

One year, as Peter was preparing for his annual Easter egg delivery, he discovered that his magical Easter eggs had gone missing. Without them, he wouldn't be able to bring joy and happiness to all the children on Easter morning.

Desperate to find his missing eggs, Peter set out on a treasure hunt to find them. He searched high and low, in every nook and cranny of the forest, but he couldn't find them anywhere. Just as he was about to give up hope, he heard a faint noise coming from a nearby cave.

Curious, Peter ventured inside the cave and soon found himself in a beautiful underground chamber. In the center of the chamber, he saw a large, sparkling Easter egg. As he approached it, the egg began to glow and shimmer, and a voice spoke to him.

"Peter, I am the guardian of the Easter eggs. I have hidden them here in the cave for safekeeping. But I have also placed a challenge for you. If you can solve my riddles and find all the eggs, they will be yours."

Peter was thrilled at the prospect of solving the riddles and finding his missing Easter eggs. He eagerly listened as the guardian gave him the first riddle.

"I am not alive, but I grow; I don't have lungs, but I need air; I don't have a mouth, but water kills me. What am I?"

Peter thought long and hard about the riddle, and finally, he remembered that fire needs air to grow but does not have lungs. He shouted out "Fire" and the guardian was impressed and gave him the next riddle.

The next riddle was even more challenging, but Peter was determined to find all the eggs. He solved each riddle with determination and soon, he had found all of the Easter eggs.

As he collected the last egg, the chamber began to shake, and the eggs started to glow even brighter. Suddenly, the eggs transformed into a beautiful golden color, and the guardian appeared before Peter once again.

"Well done, Peter," the guardian said. "You have proven yourself to be a true Easter Bunny. These eggs are now yours, and they possess a special magic that will bring joy and happiness to all the children on Easter morning."

With a heart full of gratitude, Peter thanked the guardian and made his way back to his burrow, where his wife and children were waiting for him. He presented them with the magical Easter eggs and they were all amazed by their beauty and magic.

From that day on, Peter's Easter egg deliveries were the most sought-after and beloved in the land, and the magic of the Easter eggs brought happiness and joy to children everywhere.